Personal
Achievement

Personal Achievement
rian Tracy

Saeed Book Bank
Importers & Distributors, Booksellers & Publishers
F-7, Jinnah Super Market, Islamabad-Pakistan.
Tel : 92-51-2651656-9, Fax : 92-51-2651660
E-mail : sales@saeedbookbank.com
Arbab Road, Peshawar Cantt. Pakistan.
Tel : 92-91-5273761, 5285724
Fax : 92-91-5275801, 5274081
E-mail : sbb@pes.comsata.net.pk
Web : www.saeedbookbank.com

Personal
Achievement

Brian Tracy

JAICO PUBLISHING HOUSE
Ahmedabad Bangalore Bhopal Chennai
Delhi Hyderabad Kolkata Lucknow Mumbai

Published by Jaico Publishing House
A-2 Jash Chambers, 7-A Sir Phirozshah Mehta Road
Fort, Mumbai - 400 001
jaicopub@jaicobooks.com
www.jaicobooks.com

© Career Press

Published in arrangement with
Career Press, Inc.
3 Tice Road, Franklin Lakes
NJ 07417, U.S.A.

PERSONAL ACHIEVEMENT
ISBN 81-7224-711-7

First Jaico Impression: 1999
Seventh Jaico Impression (Enlarged Edition): 2008
Eighth Jaico Impression: 2010

No part of this book may be reproduced or utilized in
any form or by any means, electronic or
mechanical including photocopying, recording or by
any information storage and retrieval system,
without permission in writing from the publishers.

Printed by
Kumar Offset Printers
381, F.I.E. Patparganj Ind. Area, Delhi-92.

1

Personal Achievement

Imagine your life is perfect in every respect; what would it look like?

There are no limits on what you can achieve with your life, except the limits you accept in your mind.

It doesn't matter where you're coming from; all that matters is where you are going.

You have great, untapped reserves of potential within you. Your job is to release them.

Brian Tracy

Life is like a combination lock; your goal is to find the right numbers, in the right order, so you can have anything you want.

If you do the right things in the right way, you will get whatever results you desire.

Everything you do in life is either to get love, or to compensate for lack of love.

Your most valuable asset can be your willingness to persist longer than anyone else.

Personal Achievement

Your inner voice will ultimately guide you to say and do the right things at the right time.

Learn from the experts; you will not live long enough to figure it all out for yourself.

Nature is neutral; if you do the same things that other successful people have done, you will inevitably enjoy the same success they have.

If you want to achieve greatly in life, be a student of achievement.

Almost all your happiness in life comes from your tendency to blame someone else for something.

Decide exactly what you want in every area of your life; you can't hit a target you can't see.

Any system or blueprint for success is better than none at all. Think on paper.

Virtually anything you could ever want to be, have or do is achievable with learning and hard work.

5

Personal Achievement

Make your life a masterpiece; imagine no limitations on what you can be, have or do.

You have the ability, right now, to exceed all your previous levels of accomplishment.

If you are worried about money, it simply means that you can and should be earning more. How are you going to do it?

Make a decision today to do something wonderful with your life.

The great secret of success is that there are no secrets of success; there are only timeless principles that have proven effective throughout the centuries.

Peace of mind is the highest human good and it is your normal, natural condition. Ask yourself, "Do you want to be right, or do you want to be happy?"

Do something to move yourself toward your major goal every day.

You are successful to the degree to which you can attain your own happiness.

Personal Achievement

The kindest thing you can do for the people you care about is to become a happy, joyous person.

You can't give away something that you don't have; you can't make others happy if you are unhappy.

A positive mental attitude goes hand-in-hand with success in every area of life.

You are positive, creative and happy to the degree to which you eliminate negative emotions from your life.

Engage in "mountaintop thinking"; project forward in thought and imagine your ideal life. What does it look like?

"Only one life, that soon is past; only what's done with love will last."
—Author Unknown

Be willing to launch in faith, with no guarantees of success. This is the mark of personal greatness.

You are always free to choose what you do with your life. To make changes in your future, make new choices today.

Most of your happiness, and your unhappiness, comes with hair on top, and talks back.

Decide today to design and build the ideal relationship in your life. It's up to you.

If you were starting over today, what changes would you make in your life?

The amount you laugh in your relationships with others is the true measure of the health of your personality.

Never complain, never explain. Resist the temptation to defend yourself or make excuses.

You are only as free as your options; develop alternatives to every situation.

Time is money; continually look for ways to do things faster and better.

We live in the richest society in all of human history; are you getting your fair share?

11

Personal Achievement

To be wealthy, you must develop a burning desire for wealth and financial independence.

Decide how much you want to be earning one year, five years and ten years from today. What will you have to do to achieve these amounts?

Design your financial future in every respect, and then make a plan to achieve it.

To be truly happy, you need a clear sense of meaning and purpose in life.

An attitude of calm, confident expectation activates your creativity and unlocks your mental powers.

If necessity is the mother of invention, pain seems to be the father of learning.

You are where you are and what you are because you have decided to be there.

Make a commitment today to something bigger and more important than yourself.

Personal Achievement

Self-actualization and self-fulfilment result when you feel that you are becoming everything that you are capable of becoming.

Happiness is the progressive realization of a worthy ideal.

To perform at your best, you need to know who you are and why you think and feel the way you do.

The success you are enjoying today is the result of the price you have paid in the past.

You are not what you think you are; but what you think, you are! You always behave, on the outside, in a manner consistent with your self-concept, on the inside.

Life is hard; it always has been and it always will be. Accepting this reality somehow makes it easier.

You can learn anything you need to learn to achieve any goal you can set for yourself.

15

Personal Achievement

If you change your thinking, you change your life.

Destructive criticism in childhood causes you to fear failure and rejection as an adult.

Failure is an absolute prerequisite for success. You learn to succeed by failing.

Action-orientation, the willingness to move fast when opportunity presents itself, is the key quality for success in every area.

All change in your life comes when your mind collides with a new idea.

Anything you can hold in your mind on a continuing basis, you can have.

Set peace of mind as your highest goal and organize your entire life around it.

You are a potential genius; there is no problem you cannot solve, and no answer you cannot find somewhere.

Personal Achievement

Your multi-dimensional brain is influenced by everything you see, hear, read, smell, touch, feel or say. Be careful.

Take charge! You feel positive about yourself to the exact degree to which you feel you are in control of your own life.

For every effect in your life, there is a specific cause. There is a reason for everything.

Decide in advance to use every adversity or setback as a spur to greater effort.

Set high goals and standards for yourself; resist the temptation of the comfort zone.

Live in harmony with your highest values and your innermost convictions. Never compromise.

If there is anything you want in life, find out how others have achieved it and then do the same things they did.

Thoughts are causes and conditions are effects. You are creating your current life with your present thinking.

Personal Achievement

If there is something in your life you do not want, find the cause and remove it.

The one thing over which you have complete control is your thinking; use it well.

Setting deadlines for your goals activates your subconscious mind and reinforces your determination.

To be successful, do what other successful people have done and keep doing it until you get the same results.

You learn to love others by doing loving things with and for them.

Smile. Everyone you meet is carrying a heavy load.

Whatever you believe, with conviction, becomes your reality, whether or not it is true or false.

You must become the person you want to be on the inside before you see the appearance of this person on the outside.

Personal Achievement

Develop a benevolent world view; look for the good in the people and circumstances around you.

The biggest mental roadblocks that you will ever have to overcome are those represented by your self-limiting beliefs.

If you conduct yourself as though you expect to be successful and happy, you will seldom be disappointed.

You can judge the validity of any idea or concept by asking, "Is this true for me?"

If you are starting over today, what would you do differently? Whatever your answer, start doing it now.

Theodore Roosevelt said, "Do what you can, with what you have, right where you are." This is great advice.

Start every morning by saying, "I believe something wonderful is going to happen to me today." Repeat it over and over.

Successful people are very clear about who they are and what they want.

23

Personal Achievement

Your incredible brain can take you from rags to riches, from loneliness to popularity and from depression to happiness and joy—if you use it properly.

Everything you do is triggered by an emotion of either desire or fear.

Your brain has more than 100 billion cells, each connected to at least 20,000 other cells. The possible combinations are greater than the number of molecules in the known universe.

Write out your goals on 3 × 5 index cards; review them twice each day.

You are in the people business, no matter what you do or where you do it.

Become an "inverse paranoid," someone who believes that the universe is conspiring to do you good.

Quickly say, "That's good!" to every setback and adversity, and then find out what is good about it.

Personal Achievement

Everything you have in your life you have attracted to yourself because of the person you are.

You can have more, be more and do more because you can change the person you are.

You must be absolutely clear about your goal, but be flexible about the process of achieving it.

Two men looked out through prison bars; one saw the mud, the other saw the stars."

You are where you are and what you are because of what you believe yourself to be. Change your beliefs and you change your reality.

You have gone as far as you can today with your current level of knowledge and skill.

Thought is creative. You create your entire life with your thoughts, hour by hour and minute by minute.

Personal Achievement

Your true beliefs and values are only and always expressed in your actions, especially what you do under pressure.

"Circumstances do not make the man; they merely reveal him to himself."

—Epictetus

It is when you finally learn that your fears are all in your mind that your real life begins.

It is not failure itself that holds you back; it is the fear of failure that paralyzes you.

"Courage is rightly considered the foremost of the virtues, for upon it, all others depend."
—Winston Churchill

You inevitably attract into your life people and circumstances in harmony with your dominant thoughts.

Be positive; refuse to complain, condemn or criticize anyone or anything.

Your outer world tends to be a reflection of your inner world.

Personal Achievement

The core of your personality is your self-esteem, "How much you like yourself." The more you like and respect yourself, the better you do at everything you attempt.

"Failure is merely another opportunity to more intelligently begin again."
—Henry Ford

Personality development is the process of building and maintaining high levels of self-esteem. You can change your performance by changing the way you think about yourself in that area.

Many of the most successful men and women in the world never graduated from college. They attended the "school of life" instead.

Think continually in terms of the rewards of success rather than the penalties of failure.

You develop the habit of courage by acting courageously whenever you are afraid. Do the thing you fear and the death of fear is certain.

Personal Achievement

Be future-oriented. When facing any problem, ask, "Where do we go from here?"

Your self-image controls your performance; see yourself as confident and in complete control.

Take control of your suggestive environment and only let in the words, images and ideas you desire.

Good habits are hard to form but easy to live with; bad habits are easy to form but hard to live with.

Self-esteem and self-love are the opposites of fear; the more you like yourself, the less you fear anything.

To remain positive and confident, think about your goals all the time.

Do you want to increase your rate of success? Then double your rate of failure.

Make strong, affirmative statements to reinforce new, positive habit patterns of thought and behaviour.

Personal Achievement

You can only have as much love for yourself as you can express to others.

What one great thing would you dare to dream if you knew you could not fail?

Your life today is the result of all of your choices and decisions in the past. When you make new choices, you create a new future.

Continually bombard your mind with thoughts, words, pictures and people consistent with the person you want to be and the goals you want to achieve.

You can develop any habit of thought or behaviour that you consider desirable or necessary.

Everything around you in the material world only has the meaning that you give to it with your thoughts.

You cannot control what happens; you can only control the way you respond to what happens.

You are inordinately influenced by those whose love and respect you most value.

Personal Achievement

Think continually about what you want, not about the things you fear.

"The greatest revolution of my life is the discovery that individuals can change the outer aspects of their lives by changing the inner attitudes of their minds."
—William James

Create your own poster, covered with pictures of the things you want to acquire. All improvement in your life begins with an improvement in your mental pictures.

You are continually evolving and growing in the direction of your dominant thoughts.

Go on a 21-day PMA (Positive Mental Attitude) diet; think and talk about only the things you want for three weeks. This is not easy.

Excellence is not a destination; it is a continuous journey that never ends.

Speaking aloud to yourself in a positive, confident way builds your self-confidence and improves your performance.

Personal Achievement

Affirming your desired goals is a way of telling the truth in advance.

Keep your conversation throughout the day consistent with what you really want to happen.

Visualize your goals and ideals continually, to influence your subconscious mind.

Act the part; walk and talk exactly as if you were already the person you want to be.

Say the words, "I like myself!" over and over, 50 times a day.

Feed your mind with mental protein, not mental candy. Read, listen to and watch positive, uplifting material.

Ignorance breeds fear; the more you learn about your subject, the less fear it holds for you.

The people you choose to associate with will determine your success as much as any other factor.

Personal Achievement

Associate with positive people, and get away from negative people.

The more you teach positive ideas to others, the better you learn them yourself.

Decide what you want, and then act as if it were impossible to fail.

Stop talking about the problem and start thinking about the solution.

Take a deep breath, relax and imagine yourself exactly as you wish to be.

Feeling listless? Make a list! Write down 10 things that you want to achieve in the next year.

What you think about most of the time is what you become.

Don't go out and just have a good day; instead, make it a good day!

Act with purpose, courage, confidence, competence and intelligence until these qualities "lock in" to your subconscious mind.

Personal Achievement

Any idea or thought that you accept as true will be accepted as a command by your subconscious mind.

Your conscious mind can only hold one thought at a time, positive or negative. Which is it going to be?

Your mind will make you rich or poor, depending on the uses you put it to.

Your success will be largely determined by your ability to concentrate single-mindedly on one thing at a time.

Close your eyes, take seven deep breaths, and then visualize your most important goal as already a reality.

Play gentle, classical music when you read, study or think about your goals.

Emotionalize your mental images; your mental movies are your previews of life's coming attractions.

Wisdom is an equal combination of experience plus reflection. Take time to think about your life.

Personal Achievement

Imagine that you are already the very best in your field; how would you behave differently? The fear of failure is the greatest single obstacle to success in adult life.

You can never rise higher than your expectations of yourself. Expect the best!

There are no extra human beings; you are here on this earth to do something special with your life.

Everything in your life happens for a reason; there are no accidents.

Your ability to set goals and to make plans for their accomplishment is the master skill of success.

You can accomplish virtually any goal you set for yourself, as long as the goal is clear and you persist long enough.

True happiness and fulfilment come when you feel that you are making a valuable contribution to your world. What is yours?

Goals are the fuel in the furnace of achievement.

Personal Achievement

It is not what you say, or wish, or hope or intend, it is only what you do that counts.

You are only happy when you are working toward a clear, specific goal of your own choosing.

As you change the way you think on the inside, people and circumstances will change for you on the outside.

Your subconscious mind cannot tell the difference between a real experience and one that you vividly imagine. Fool it.

Each of us must develop an area of excellence where he performs better than almost anyone else.

The only limitation on your ability is your level of desire; how badly do you want it?

"Intensity of purpose" is the distinguishing characteristic of high performing men and women.

The tendency to follow the path of least resistance guarantees failure in life.

Personal Achievement

You must decide exactly what is it you want in life; no one can do this for you.

An attitude of positive expectation is the mark of the superior personality.

Clear goals allow you to control the direction of change in your life.

Resolve that you will respond with a positive, optimistic and cheerful mental attitude in every situation.

Combine your mental images with the emotion of desire to accelerate their realization.

You are already achieving every goal you are setting for yourself. Are you happy with your results?

Determine the price you are going to have to pay to achieve your goal, and then resolve to pay that price.

Look for something beneficial in every event that you can turn to your advantage.

Personal Achievement

Success is a numbers game; there is a direct relationship between the number of things you try and your probability of ultimately succeeding.

Think about your goals at every opportunity throughout the day.

Start with a picture of your goal as already achieved in the future, and work back to the present. Imagine the steps that you would have taken to get from where you are now to where you want to be.

Ideas are a dime a dozen, but people to put them into effect are extremely rare.

If you swing hard enough and often enough you must eventually hit a home run.

Selecting your major definite purpose in life is the starting point of personal greatness.

Keep your goals confidential; only tell people who are sympathetic to you, and who have goals of their own.

Personal Achievement

Success equals goals; all else is commentary.

Success comes when you do what you love to do and commit to being the best in your field.

Your greatest opportunity for success probably lies right under your own feet, your own acres of diamonds.

If you won a million dollars' cash, what work would you choose to do for the foreseeable future?

Opportunities usually come dressed in work clothes.

Organize your life around your values; what do you believe in and stand for?

Imagine no limitations; decide what's right and desirable before you decide what's possible.

Write down every goal you could want to accomplish in the next 10 years, then choose the most important one.

Personal Achievement

To enjoy perfect health, define what your life would be like if you already had it. Then do what you need to do to acquire it.

You only have to succeed the last time.

Goal setting is a science learned only by study, practice and application.

The people you love, and who love you, are the real measure of how well you are doing as a human being.

If you were absolutely guaranteed of success in any one thing, what one goal would you set for yourself?

"What doesn't kill me makes me stronger."
—Friedrich Nietzsche

What have you always wanted to do but been afraid to attemtp? What fears are holding you back?

The thrill of achievement comes from overcoming adversity in the accomplishment of an important goal.

Personal Achievement

Before you can achieve big goals, major efforts are necessary.

The north wind made the Vikings.

Make a list of all the ways that you will personally benefit from achieving your goal.

Character is the ability to carry through on a resolution long after the emotion with which the resolution was made has passed.

Decisiveness is a common characteristic of all successful men and women.

Intense, burning desire is the motivational force that enables you to overcome any obstacle and achieve almost any goal.

If every possible obstacle must first be overcome, nothing will ever get done.

The simple act of writing down a goal and making a written plan for its accomplishment moves you to the top 3 percent.

Personal Achievement

Nurture your faith and belief until they deepen into an absolute conviction that your goal is attainable.

Make your goals both realistic and achievable.

Those who do not have goals are doomed forever to work for those who do.

The price of success must be paid in full, in advance.

Completely unrealistic goals are a form of self-delusion, and you cannot delude yourself into success.

The more reasons you have for achieving your goal, the more determined you will become.

What is the biggest single obstacle that stands between you and your goal, right now?

What additional knowledge and skill will you need to achieve your goal? Where can you acquire them?

Personal Achievement

Make a plan, a list organized by priority, to achieve your goal.

"Stick to the fight when you're hardest hit; it's when things seem worst that you must not quit!"

—Anonymous

Rewrite your major goals every day, in the present tense, exactly as if they already existed.

Your superconscious mind will guide you to do and say exactly the right thing in every situation.

The disease of excusitis is invariably fatal to success.

"We lie in the lap of an immense intelligence that responds to our every need."
—Ralph Waldo Emerson

You are surrounded by a universal mind that contains all the intelligence, ideas and knowledge that have ever existed.

Make firm decisions about the things you want; burn your mental bridges behind you.

Personal Achievement

Your superconscious mind automatically and continuously solves every problem on the way to your goal.

Superior people take both the credit and the blame for everything that happens to them.

Resolve to accept the worst, should it occur. Now you can stop worrying.

"Whenever you find something getting done, anywhere, you will find a monomaniac with a mission."
—Peter Drucker

Whenever you set a goal of any kind, you will have to grow and develop to the point where you are ready to achieve it.

If you achieve your success without being prepared for it, you'll only end up looking foolish.

Most people achieved their greatest successes one step beyond what looked like their greatest failure.

When your goals are clear, you will come up with exactly the right answer at exactly the right time.

Personal Achievement

Self-responsibility is the core quality of the fully mature, fully functioning, self-actualizing individual.

Issue a blanket pardon. Forgive everyone who has ever hurt you in any way.

Forgiveness is a perfectly selfish act. It sets you free from the past.

View yourself as self-employed, the president of your own personal services corporation.

Whenever you feel angry or upset for any reason, neutralize the negative emotions by saying, "I am responsible!"

Eliminate worry by identifying the worst possible outcome of every situation.

Eliminating the expression of negative emotions is the starting point of rapid personal growth.

"I never hold grudges. While you're holding grudges, they're out dancing!"
—Buddy Hackett

Personal Achievement

Repentance is good for the soul; apologize for anything you have done to hurt someone else.

Love only grows by sharing. You can only have more for yourself by giving it away to others.

If you're unhappy, what is it in your life that you're not facing?

When you are younger, you worry about what people think about you. When you are older, you realize that no one was ever thinking about you at all.

Most unhappiness is caused by a lack of clear meaning and purpose in your life.

There is always a price you can pay to be free of any unhappiness, and you always know what it is.

Overconcern for the approval of others can paralyze your ability to take effective action.

Denial of some unpleasant reality lies at the core of most stress, unhappiness and psychosomatic illness.

Personal Achievement

Once you start an important job, stay with it until it's 100-percent complete.

Winding up "unfinished business" with another person can give you a great burst of positive energy.

Which goal, if you accomplish it, will do more to help you achieve all your other goals?

What would you do, how would you spend your time, if you learned today that you only had six months to live?

Healthy, happy people are those who confront the facts of their lives directly.

Your personality is healthy to the degree to which you can get along with a variety of other people.

Everything you do to raise the self-esteem of others raises your own self-esteem at the same time.

Stress and unhappiness come not from situations, but from how you respond to situations.

Personal Achievement

Nobody makes you angry; you decide to use anger as a response.

The fastest way to improve your relationships is to make others feel important in every way possible.

Any thought, plan, goal or idea held continuously in your conscious mind must be brought into reality by your superconscious mind.

Practice "white magic"; listen attentively to others when they speak.

Identify and develop your unique talents and abilities, the things that make you special.

Be agreeable. It raises the self-esteem of others and makes you feel good about yourself.

Love of others begins with self-love and self-acceptance.

Develop an "attitude of gratitude." Say "thank you" to everyone for everything they do for you.

Personal Achievement

Fully 95 percent of everything you think and feel is habitual and automatic, determined by past behaviours and experiences.

The only thing that you can never have too much of is love.

The way you get along with yourself will determine how well you get along with others.

With relationships, either get in or get out. Make a total commitment, or go your own way.

The purpose of life is to develop loving relationships, and to become a totally loving person.

Treat the people in your life as though they were the most important people in the world, because they are.

Listening builds trust, the foundation of all lasting relationships.

You are just about as happy as you decide to be. Make up your mind to be a cheerful, optimistic person.

Personal Achievement

Any good that you can do, do it now. Do not delay it or forestall it, for you will not pass this way again.

Why haven't you achieved your goals yet? What are your favourite excuses, and how do they hold you back?

Make a total commitment today, to yourself, your goals and your relationships. Hold nothing back.

Become unstoppable by never stopping once you have started toward a goal that is important to you.

Successful people do not always make the right decisions, but they make their decisions right.

The more you tell people that you love them, the more you love yourself.

You only learn from feedback; the faster and more often you fail, the more rapidly you learn and succeed.

Your cybernetic brain mechanism will guide you unerringly to your goal, as long as the goal is clear.

Personal Achievement

Make a decision! If that doesn't work, make another, and another, and another. Keep doing this until you break through.

The common characteristic of self-made millionaires is that they continually work harder and smarter than the average person.

Your success in life will be in direct proportion to what you do after you've done what is expected of you.

Within every setback or obstacle there is the seed of an equal or greater advantage or benefit. Find it.

"This above all, to thine own self be true,
And it must follow as the night the day,
Thou canst not then be false to any man."
—William Shakespeare

The antidotes to fear and ignorance are desire and knowledge. Propel yourself forward by learning what you need to learn to do what you want to do.

Personal Achievement

Get out of your own way; most of your excuses for underachievement are figments of your imagination.

Knowledge is power, but only knowledge that can be applied to practical purposes in some way.

A horse that wins by a nose receives 10 times the prize money of a horse that loses by a nose. Little things mean a lot.

Practice "creative abandonment" of time-consuming activities that are no longer of importance to you.

Always work on the 20 percent of your activities that contribute 80 percent of your results. What are they?

The best songs are yet to be sung, the best stories are yet to be told, and the best years of your life lie ahead.

You are surrounded right now by unlimited opportunities disguised as insurmountable problems.

Goals that are not in writing are merely wishes or fantasies.

Personal Achievement

The future belongs to the competent; resolve to join the top 10 percent of people in your field and your future will be unlimited.

The golden rule is still the best principle for success: "Do unto others as you would have them do unto you."

You can see what is going on inside of you by looking at what is going on around you.

Luck is predictable; the harder you work, the luckier you get.

"There is a tide in the affairs of men which when taken at the flood leads on to fortune."
—William Shakespeare

"Lucky" people are simply those who think continually about what they want and then attract it into their lives.

Think of yourself as you wish to be, not as you are today.

The more positive you are when you think and work toward your goals, the faster you achieve them.

Personal Achievement

Become an unshakable optimist by thinking continually of the things you want, and by refusing to think about the things you fear.

There are no accidents; success is the result of doing the right thing, in the right way, over and over.

"You never call tell how close you are, You may be near when it seems so far."
—Anonymous

It is your attitude more than your aptitude that determines your altitude.

Time is your most precious resource; make every minute count.